BLACKJOY

A 30-DAY JOURNEY TO EMPOWERMENT & GRATITUDE

THADDEUS MILES

BLACKJOY

A 30-DAY JOURNEY TO EMPOWERMENT & GRATITUDE

THADDEUS MILES

Published by The BlackJoy Warrior Initiative.

For permission requests, email to the publisher, subject "Attention: Permissions Coordinator," at the email address below:

theblackjoywarriorinitiative@gmail.com

First Edition: 2023

WELCOME

Welcome to the 30-Day BlackJoy Journal, a personal journey of empowerment, gratitude, and self-reflection. This journal is designed to help you celebrate your BlackJoy, heritage, and culture, while also fostering personal growth and promoting positive change within your community.

Throughout this 30-day journey, you'll be guided by daily affirmations, accountability questions, and gratitude reflection questions. These prompts will encourage you to explore different aspects of your BlackJoy, from honoring your ancestors to acknowledging the achievements of fellow Black community members.

A NOTE FROM THE AUTHOR

The incomparable Maya Angelou once said, "My mission in life is not merely to survive, but to thrive; and to do so with some passion, some compassion, some humor, and some style." This quote embodies the essence of the BlackJoy concept, now in its fifth year, and the HoodFit movement, a decade strong. These initiatives have given rise to milestones like the establishment of BlackJoy Days in Massachusetts and the successful execution of the Road to Wellness 5k.

My journey of embracing BlackJoy has been transformative, particularly over the last several months. The opportunity to sit on a BlackJoy panel at the 'How to Boston While Black' summit was a moment of significant insight and learning. The dialogues with fellow panelists and the audience responses sparked a deeper understanding of our need to document our unique journeys. It was in preparation for this summit that I developed the Four BlackJoy Pillars, a framework to guide our exploration of BlackJoy.

As a photographer, I've been privileged to explore the multifaceted dimensions of BlackJoy. It's about living radiantly and unapologetically in your skin, celebrating your culture, and laughing, singing, and dancing through life's challenges. It's about feeling safe and at home in your blackness, without any obstructions.

My lens has been a witness to moments of pure, radiant BlackJoy. Each captured moment, intentional or not, is meaningful and profound. I believe it's crucial to document every part of the Black experience, not only as a form of cultural appreciation and preservation but also as a testament to the strength and resilience of our people. My work contributes to the collective narrative of the power and influence of black traditions worldwide. It is a love letter to Black people. I see you in all your glory and splendor.

This sentiment of being seen and affirmed is echoed in the South African phrase, "Sawabona." It is a sentiment that we, as Black Americans, resonate with deeply. To be seen is to have your existence validated. It is a powerful resistance against erasure, one of the most potent tools of oppression. Through my photography, I aim to illuminate the fullness of the Black narrative and map our existence.

BlackJoy, for me, is my camera in hand, embracing the magnificence inherited from the continent of Africa, one of the most potent sources of power and beauty on this earth. It is a soul-drenched knowing that I was created for a purpose and have the agency to manifest that purpose every single day I live on this earth.

Living as a Black person in Massachusetts is a unique and multifaceted experience. It involves navigating through the high and low expectations from various communities, challenging stereotypes, and finding common ground. Yet, despite these challenges, there is a sense of hope, a call to be part of an emerging change.

This journal, inspired by the concept of BlackJoy, is a tool for you to explore, celebrate, and document your unique journey. My hope is that it helps you find your BlackJoy and empowers you to share your story with the world.

In the spirit of 'Sawabona,' I see you.

– Thaddeus Miles

WHY A BLACKJOY JOURNAL?

In a world where Black individuals and communities often face adversity, discrimination, and systemic racism, it's essential to create spaces and practices that focus on celebrating the richness of Black culture and the power of BlackJoy. This journal serves as a tool to support your journey, helping you build resilience, connection, and gratitude, while also empowering you to advocate for yourself and your community.

THE FOUR PILLARS OF BLACKJOY

Building on the insights shared in the previous pages,
I've distilled the core tenets that can help navigate our journey
towards BlackJoy. These Four BlackJoy Pillars emerged from
deep introspection and continuous dialogue with our community.
Each one stands as a beacon, lighting the path towards a fuller
understanding and embodiment of BlackJoy.

1
Love and Honor Yourself

Prioritize your well-being by practicing self-care and celebrating your unique identity, culture, and accomplishments.

2
Surround Yourself with Support

Foster positivity and community by connecting with those who uplift you and by investing in the collective growth of your community.

3
Speak Your Truth with Courage

Share your experiences, opinions, and perspectives confidently and be open to growth and learning.

4
Practice Radical Self-Care and Embrace Diversity

Emphasize your physical, mental, and emotional health, and celebrate the richness of diverse cultures, histories, and experiences.

Difference Between Pillar 1 & 4:

Agreement 1 centers on the act of personal self-care and the celebration of one's unique identity. Agreement 4, on the other hand, accentuates an intense commitment to self-well-being while also highlighting the importance of recognizing and celebrating diversity. In essence, the first is about self-appreciation, while the fourth emphasizes both deep self-care and an appreciation for the broader spectrum of diverse experiences and cultures.

HOW TO USE
THIS JOURNAL

Each day, set aside some time to read the affirmation aloud, respond to the accountability question, and reflect on the gratitude question.

AFFIRMATION

Begin each day by reading the affirmation aloud. These affirmations serve as a daily reminder to embrace your BlackJoy, strength, and resilience.

ACCOUNTABILITY

The accountability questions will help you reflect on your daily actions and experiences, encouraging you to express your BlackJoy, engage with your community, and prioritize self-care.

GRATITUDE

Gratitude reflection questions invite you to pause and appreciate the aspects of your life, culture, and community that bring you joy and happiness. By cultivating gratitude, you'll foster a mindset of abundance, positivity, and growth.

Remember that there is no right or wrong way to engage with this journal. The key is to stay consistent and commit to this journey of self-discovery and growth. Be gentle with yourself, embrace the process, and allow your BlackJoy to flourish.

DAY 1

I embrace my BlackJoy and celebrate my culture with pride and love.

ACCOUNTABILITY

How did I express my BlackJoy today?

GRATITUDE

What aspect of my culture am I most grateful for?

Reflect on today's events. In detail, chronicle any particular experiences, interactions, or moments that stood out to you.

_____

_____

_____

_____

_____

_____

_____

_____

Of these moments, identify one that was especially meaningful. Why did it resonate with you? What feelings did it evoke? What about this experience are you especially grateful for?

_____

_____

_____

_____

_____

_____

_____

_____

DAY 2

I am a powerful force for positive change in my community.

What actions have I taken to uplift and empower my community today?

What recent community accomplishment am I most grateful for?

Reflect on today's events. In detail, chronicle any particular experiences, interactions, or moments that stood out to you.

_____

_____

_____

_____

_____

_____

_____

_____

Of these moments, identify one that was especially meaningful. Why did it resonate with you? What feelings did it evoke? What about this experience are you especially grateful for?

_____

_____

_____

_____

_____

_____

_____

_____

DAY 3

AFFIRMATION

I honor my ancestors by living my life with purpose and resilience.

ACCOUNTABILITY

How did I honor my ancestors today?

GRATITUDE

What family traditions am I grateful for?

Reflect on today's events. In detail, chronicle any particular experiences, interactions, or moments that stood out to you.

_____

_____

_____

_____

_____

_____

_____

_____

Of these moments, identify one that was especially meaningful. Why did it resonate with you? What feelings did it evoke? What about this experience are you especially grateful for?

_____

_____

_____

_____

_____

_____

_____

_____

DAY 4

I am a beacon of light, sharing my BlackJoy with others.

How did I share my joy with others today?

Who in my life has been a source of BlackJoy, and why am I grateful for them?

Reflect on today's events. In detail, chronicle any particular experiences, interactions, or moments that stood out to you.

_____

_____

_____

_____

_____

_____

_____

_____

Of these moments, identify one that was especially meaningful. Why did it resonate with you? What feelings did it evoke? What about this experience are you especially grateful for?

_____

_____

_____

_____

_____

_____

_____

_____

DAY 5

I cultivate my self-worth and nurture my soul with self-care and love.

ACCOUNTABILITY

How did I practice self-care today?

GRATITUDE

What do I love about myself?

Reflect on today's events. In detail, chronicle any particular experiences, interactions, or moments that stood out to you.

_____

_____

_____

_____

_____

_____

_____

_____

Of these moments, identify one that was especially meaningful. Why did it resonate with you? What feelings did it evoke? What about this experience are you especially grateful for?

_____

_____

_____

_____

_____

_____

_____

_____

DAY 6

My creativity is a reflection of my BlackJoy and heritage.

How did I express my creativity today?

What creative outlet am I most grateful for?

Reflect on today's events. In detail, chronicle any particular experiences, interactions, or moments that stood out to you.

_____

_____

_____

_____

_____

_____

_____

_____

Of these moments, identify one that was especially meaningful. Why did it resonate with you? What feelings did it evoke? What about this experience are you especially grateful for?

_____

_____

_____

_____

_____

_____

_____

_____

DAY 7

I am surrounded by a loving and supportive community.

How did I strengthen my connections with my community today?

Which supportive person in my life am I most grateful for?

Reflect on today's events. In detail, chronicle any particular experiences, interactions, or moments that stood out to you.

_____

_____

_____

_____

_____

_____

_____

_____

Of these moments, identify one that was especially meaningful. Why did it resonate with you? What feelings did it evoke? What about this experience are you especially grateful for?

_____

_____

_____

_____

_____

_____

_____

_____

ONE WEEK DOWN!

Congratulations on completing your first week of the BlackJoy Journal.

Every word you've written is a testament to your commitment and desire to embrace BlackJoy. Your dedication to exploring, understanding, and celebrating your unique journey is commendable.

"

EVERY PAGE TURNED IS A STEP CLOSER
TO A DEEPER UNDERSTANDING OF
ONESELF. CHERISH THIS JOURNEY;
IT'S YOURS AND ONLY YOURS.
– TM

DAY 8

AFFIRMATION

I have the power to create a brighter future for myself and my community.

ACCOUNTABILITY

How did I contribute to a better future today?

GRATITUDE

What opportunities am I grateful for?

Reflect on today's events. In detail, chronicle any particular experiences, interactions, or moments that stood out to you.

_____

_____

_____

_____

_____

_____

_____

Of these moments, identify one that was especially meaningful. Why did it resonate with you? What feelings did it evoke? What about this experience are you especially grateful for?

_____

_____

_____

_____

_____

_____

_____

DAY 9

I am a force of positivity, love, and wisdom in the face of adversity.

How did I overcome a challenge today?

What lesson from a difficult experience am I grateful for?

Reflect on today's events. In detail, chronicle any particular experiences, interactions, or moments that stood out to you.

_____

_____

_____

_____

_____

_____

_____

_____

Of these moments, identify one that was especially meaningful. Why did it resonate with you? What feelings did it evoke? What about this experience are you especially grateful for?

_____

_____

_____

_____

_____

_____

_____

_____

DAY 10

My voice matters and my story is important.

How did I use my voice to make a difference today?

What opportunities have I had to share my story, and why am I grateful for them?

Reflect on today's events. In detail, chronicle any particular experiences, interactions, or moments that stood out to you.

_____

_____

_____

_____

_____

_____

_____

_____

Of these moments, identify one that was especially meaningful. Why did it resonate with you? What feelings did it evoke? What about this experience are you especially grateful for?

_____

_____

_____

_____

_____

_____

_____

DAY 11

I celebrate the beauty and diversity of Black culture.

How did I learn about or appreciate a different aspect of Black culture today?

What new cultural discovery am I grateful for?

Reflect on today's events. In detail, chronicle any particular experiences, interactions, or moments that stood out to you.

_____

_____

_____

_____

_____

_____

_____

_____

Of these moments, identify one that was especially meaningful. Why did it resonate with you? What feelings did it evoke? What about this experience are you especially grateful for?

_____

_____

_____

_____

_____

_____

_____

_____

DAY 12

I am committed to dismantling racism and promoting equality.

How did I take a stand against racism or injustice today?

What progress am I grateful for in the fight for justice and equality?

Reflect on today's events. In detail, chronicle any particular experiences, interactions, or moments that stood out to you.

_____

_____

_____

_____

_____

_____

_____

_____

Of these moments, identify one that was especially meaningful. Why did it resonate with you? What feelings did it evoke? What about this experience are you especially grateful for?

_____

_____

_____

_____

_____

_____

_____

_____

DAY 13

I honor the achievements and contributions of Black people throughout history.

What did I learn about a Black historical figure or event today?

What historical achievement by a Black individual am I most grateful for?

Reflect on today's events. In detail, chronicle any particular experiences, interactions, or moments that stood out to you.

_____

_____

_____

_____

_____

_____

_____

Of these moments, identify one that was especially meaningful. Why did it resonate with you? What feelings did it evoke? What about this experience are you especially grateful for?

_____

_____

_____

_____

_____

_____

_____

DAY 14

My BlackJoy is a source of strength and inspiration for others.

How did my BlackJoy inspire someone else today?

Who has been a source of inspiration in my life, and why am I grateful for them?

Reflect on today's events. In detail, chronicle any particular experiences, interactions, or moments that stood out to you.

_____

_____

_____

_____

_____

_____

_____

Of these moments, identify one that was especially meaningful. Why did it resonate with you? What feelings did it evoke? What about this experience are you especially grateful for?

_____

_____

_____

_____

_____

_____

_____

HALFWAY THERE!

Two weeks in – look how far you've come!

Your consistency is making an impact, building a bridge between self-awareness and self-celebration. Continue to pour your heart onto these pages, for therein lies the beauty of your unique story.

"

WITH EACH ENTRY, WE NOT ONLY
DOCUMENT OUR STORIES, BUT WE
WEAVE THE FABRIC OF OUR LEGACY.
KEEP WEAVING, FOR THE TAPESTRY IS
BECOMING MAGNIFICENT.
– TM

DAY 15

I am dedicated to the continued growth and development of my community.

How did I support the growth of my community today?

What community resources or programs am I grateful for?

Reflect on today's events. In detail, chronicle any particular experiences, interactions, or moments that stood out to you.

_____

_____

_____

_____

_____

_____

_____

_____

Of these moments, identify one that was especially meaningful. Why did it resonate with you? What feelings did it evoke? What about this experience are you especially grateful for?

_____

_____

_____

_____

_____

_____

_____

DAY 16

AFFIRMATION

I am a living testament to the resilience and strength of my ancestors.

ACCOUNTABILITY

I am a living testament to the resilience and strength of my ancestors.

GRATITUDE

I am a living testament to the resilience and strength of my ancestors.

Reflect on today's events. In detail, chronicle any particular experiences, interactions, or moments that stood out to you.

_____

_____

_____

_____

_____

_____

_____

_____

Of these moments, identify one that was especially meaningful. Why did it resonate with you? What feelings did it evoke? What about this experience are you especially grateful for?

_____

_____

_____

_____

_____

_____

_____

DAY 17

AFFIRMATION

I seek and create spaces where my BlackJoy can flourish.

ACCOUNTABILITY

I seek and create spaces where my BlackJoy can flourish.

GRATITUDE

What safe and nurturing spaces am I grateful for?

Reflect on today's events. In detail, chronicle any particular experiences, interactions, or moments that stood out to you.

_____

_____

_____

_____

_____

_____

_____

_____

Of these moments, identify one that was especially meaningful. Why did it resonate with you? What feelings did it evoke? What about this experience are you especially grateful for?

_____

_____

_____

_____

_____

_____

_____

_____

DAY 18

I honor and celebrate the Black artists, musicians, and creators who inspire me.

How did I support or engage with Black art, music, or other creative works today?

Which Black artist, musician, or creator am I most grateful for and why?

Reflect on today's events. In detail, chronicle any particular experiences, interactions, or moments that stood out to you.

_____

_____

_____

_____

_____

_____

_____

_____

Of these moments, identify one that was especially meaningful. Why did it resonate with you? What feelings did it evoke? What about this experience are you especially grateful for?

_____

_____

_____

_____

_____

_____

_____

DAY 19

I am deserving of happiness, love, and success.

ACCOUNTABILITY

I am deserving of happiness, love, and success.

GRATITUDE

What successes or accomplishments am I grateful for?

Reflect on today's events. In detail, chronicle any particular experiences, interactions, or moments that stood out to you.

_____

_____

_____

_____

_____

_____

_____

_____

Of these moments, identify one that was especially meaningful. Why did it resonate with you? What feelings did it evoke? What about this experience are you especially grateful for?

_____

_____

_____

_____

_____

_____

_____

DAY 20

I am a leader and a role model, inspiring others with my BlackJoy.

I am a leader and a role model, inspiring others with my BlackJoy.

I am a leader and a role model, inspiring others with my BlackJoy.

Reflect on today's events. In detail, chronicle any particular experiences, interactions, or moments that stood out to you.

_____

_____

_____

_____

_____

_____

_____

_____

Of these moments, identify one that was especially meaningful. Why did it resonate with you? What feelings did it evoke? What about this experience are you especially grateful for?

_____

_____

_____

_____

_____

_____

_____

DAY 21

I embrace my unique talents and gifts, using them to spread BlackJoy.

How did I use my unique talents or gifts today to uplift myself or others?

What talent or gift am I most grateful for, and why?

Reflect on today's events. In detail, chronicle any particular experiences, interactions, or moments that stood out to you.

_____

_____

_____

_____

_____

_____

_____

Of these moments, identify one that was especially meaningful. Why did it resonate with you? What feelings did it evoke? What about this experience are you especially grateful for?

_____

_____

_____

_____

_____

_____

_____

THREE WEEKS STRONG!

Three weeks down and just a few more days to go!

Your dedication to this journey of self-discovery and celebration is inspiring. Remember, every reflection, thought, and memory you've captured is a beacon of your growth and evolution.

"

AS THE FINAL PAGES APPROACH,
REMEMBER THAT THIS IS NOT AN ENDING,
BUT A THRESHOLD. EMBRACE THE
HORIZON WITH THE SAME PASSION AND
COMMITMENT YOU'VE SHOWN SO FAR.
– TM

DAY 22

I seek out and create connections with other Black individuals and communities.

I seek out and create connections with other Black individuals and communities.

I seek out and create connections with other Black individuals and communities.

Reflect on today's events. In detail, chronicle any particular experiences, interactions, or moments that stood out to you.

_____

_____

_____

_____

_____

_____

_____

_____

Of these moments, identify one that was especially meaningful. Why did it resonate with you? What feelings did it evoke? What about this experience are you especially grateful for?

_____

_____

_____

_____

_____

_____

_____

_____

DAY 23

My mental, emotional, and physical well-being is a priority in my life.

How did I prioritize my mental, emotional, or physical well-being today?

What aspects of my well-being am I most grateful for?

Reflect on today's events. In detail, chronicle any particular experiences, interactions, or moments that stood out to you.

_____

_____

_____

_____

_____

_____

_____

_____

Of these moments, identify one that was especially meaningful. Why did it resonate with you? What feelings did it evoke? What about this experience are you especially grateful for?

_____

_____

_____

_____

_____

_____

_____

DAY 24

I am dedicated to learning and growing in my journey towards BlackJoy.

What new knowledge or skill did I acquire today in my pursuit of BlackJoy?

What learning experience am I most grateful for?

Reflect on today's events. In detail, chronicle any particular experiences, interactions, or moments that stood out to you.

_____

_____

_____

_____

_____

_____

_____

_____

Of these moments, identify one that was especially meaningful. Why did it resonate with you? What feelings did it evoke? What about this experience are you especially grateful for?

_____

_____

_____

_____

_____

_____

_____

_____

DAY 25

I celebrate the successes and achievements of my fellow Black community members.

How did I acknowledge or celebrate someone else's achievement today?

Whose success or achievement am I most grateful for, and why?

Reflect on today's events. In detail, chronicle any particular experiences, interactions, or moments that stood out to you.

_____

_____

_____

_____

_____

_____

_____

_____

Of these moments, identify one that was especially meaningful. Why did it resonate with you? What feelings did it evoke? What about this experience are you especially grateful for?

_____

_____

_____

_____

_____

_____

_____

_____

DAY 26

I am committed to healing and nurturing my spirit through self-reflection.

What self-reflection practices did I engage in today?

What moments of self-reflection am I most grateful for?

Reflect on today's events. In detail, chronicle any particular experiences, interactions, or moments that stood out to you.

_____

_____

_____

_____

_____

_____

_____

_____

Of these moments, identify one that was especially meaningful. Why did it resonate with you? What feelings did it evoke? What about this experience are you especially grateful for?

_____

_____

_____

_____

_____

_____

_____

DAY 27

I recognize and appreciate the BlackJoy in everyday moments.

What everyday moments brought me BlackJoy today?

What simple joys am I grateful for?

Reflect on today's events. In detail, chronicle any particular experiences, interactions, or moments that stood out to you.

_____

_____

_____

_____

_____

_____

_____

_____

Of these moments, identify one that was especially meaningful. Why did it resonate with you? What feelings did it evoke? What about this experience are you especially grateful for?

_____

_____

_____

_____

_____

_____

_____

DAY 28

AFFIRMATION

I am an advocate for myself and others, championing BlackJoy in all areas of life.

ACCOUNTABILITY

How did I advocate for myself or someone else today?

GRATITUDE

What advocacy efforts or achievements am I most grateful for?

Reflect on today's events. In detail, chronicle any particular experiences, interactions, or moments that stood out to you.

_____

_____

_____

_____

_____

_____

_____

Of these moments, identify one that was especially meaningful. Why did it resonate with you? What feelings did it evoke? What about this experience are you especially grateful for?

_____

_____

_____

_____

_____

_____

_____

DAY 29

My faith and spirituality nourish my BlackJoy and guide my journey.

How did I connect with my faith or spirituality today?

What aspects of my faith or spirituality am I most grateful for?

Reflect on today's events. In detail, chronicle any particular experiences, interactions, or moments that stood out to you.

_____

_____

_____

_____

_____

_____

_____

_____

Of these moments, identify one that was especially meaningful. Why did it resonate with you? What feelings did it evoke? What about this experience are you especially grateful for?

_____

_____

_____

_____

_____

_____

_____

DAY 30

I am proud of my progress and growth throughout this BlackJoy journey.

How have I grown throughout this 30-day journey?

What personal growth or progress am I most grateful for?

Reflect on today's events. In detail, chronicle any particular experiences, interactions, or moments that stood out to you.

_____

_____

_____

_____

_____

_____

_____

_____

Of these moments, identify one that was especially meaningful. Why did it resonate with you? What feelings did it evoke? What about this experience are you especially grateful for?

_____

_____

_____

_____

_____

_____

_____

YOUR JOURNEY CONTINUES...

CONGRATULATIONS ON COMPLETING YOUR 30-DAY BLACKJOY JOURNAL.

Over the past month, you've ventured deep within, embracing your heritage, emotions, and the uniqueness that defines you. Each entry stands as a testament to your resilience, growth, and the radiant BlackJoy that courses through your spirit.

While these pages may be finite, your journey is boundless. The act of journaling is not just about reflection but about continuous evolution. Your story is still unfolding, and there are countless pages yet to be written.

Forge Your Path

As you tread onwards, mold your journaling process to fit your evolving narrative. Innovate with your daily prompts, delve deeper with affirmations, or venture into novel techniques that speak to your soul. Your growth is dynamic, and so should be your journaling approach.

Cultivate Your Tribe

Share the beauty and power of this introspective journey with others. Together, you can build a vibrant community where BlackJoy is celebrated, nurtured, and amplified. Lean on each other, inspire one another, and collectively rejoice in the tapestry of experiences that each one brings.

Your journey with BlackJoy is an everlasting symphony, each note resounding with power and purpose. Keep the melody going, honor your voice, and let the world bear witness to the endless expanse of your BlackJoy.